RELIGION IN WOOD

RELIGION IN WOOD

A BOOK OF SHAKER FURNITURE

BY EDWARD DEMING ANDREWS
AND FAITH ANDREWS

INDIANA UNIVERSITY PRESS

BLOOMINGTON AND LONDON

This book is affectionately dedicated to our children

DAVID VOLK ANDREWS

ANN ANDREWS KANE

who shared our Shaker friendships and the joys of collecting

INTRODUCTION

BY THOMAS MERTON

Prepare the furniture, O Lambeth, in thy pitying looms!
The curtains, woven tears and sighs, wrought into lovely forms
For comfort: there the secret furniture of Jerusalem's chamber
   is wrought.
Lambeth, the Bride, the Lamb's Wife loveth thee:
Thou art one with her, and knowest not of self in thy supreme
   joy.
Go on, builders in hope, tho' Jerusalem wanders far away
Without the gate of Los, among the dark Satanic wheels.
                WILLIAM BLAKE, *Jerusalem,* i

As the work of William Blake comes to be better understood and as the rich store of unpublished Shaker material is studied and brought to light, we will doubtless see that they have much in common. Blake was, of course, a contemporary of the first Shakers. Though he almost certainly had nothing to do with them, his *Jerusalem* was written about the time the Shaker villages were being built in New England, Ohio, and Kentucky, and the Shaker "style" was developing in craftsmanship. The Shaker's "religion in wood" (surely an inspired title) is an expression of a profoundly religious creativity very like that which moved Blake to write and engrave.

We know now that Blake's apparently wild and hermetic theology is not as incoherent as it was once believed to be, even though it is not always orthodox! We know also that the Shakers were something more than a community of eccentrics who had escaped from the world because they could not get along in it. If the Shakers are appreciated today (and in some quarters they are well-loved and their contribution to American culture is rightly evaluated) this is due in part to the work of Edward Deming Andrews who better than anyone else, caught their true spirit, and who interpreted it to the rest of us. This present book is a last and most eloquent word of Dr. Andrews, and in some sense a crowning and summing up of his whole work on Shaker craftsmanship and spirituality. Some time before his death in June 1964, Dr. Andrews had asked me for a preface. As a personal tribute to him I will try, in this meditation on the Shaker aesthetic, to capture something of its deep religious and "monastic" quality. Though it would be easy (as Dr. Andrews himself has shown) to approach them through the Rule of St. Benedict, I have chosen rather to look at the Shakers in the light of the artist and poet, William Blake.

It is no exaggeration to say that the simple and "lovely forms" which emerged from the fire of Shaker religious inspiration had something to do with what Blake called "the secret furniture of Jerusalem's chamber."

Neither the Shakers nor Blake would be disturbed at the thought that a work-a-day bench, cupboard, or table might also and at the same time be furniture in and for heaven: did not Blake protest mightily at the blindness of "single vision" which saw only the outward and material surface of reality, not its inner and spiritual "form" and the still more spiritual "force" from which the form proceeds? These, for Blake, were not different realities. They are one. And the "fourfold vision" of religious and creative "imagination" (more akin to prophetic vision than to phantasy) was needed if one were to be a "whole man," capable of seeing reality in its totality, and thus dwelling and expanding spiritually in "the four regions of human majesty."

> Now I a fourfold vision see
> And a fourfold vision is given to me;
> 'Tis fourfold in my supreme delight
> And threefold in soft Beulah's night
> And twofold always. May God up keep
> From single vision and Newton's sleep!

The Shaker inspiration was communal. The originality of Shaker forms, that is to say the particular development which the craftsmanship of New England and New York in the 18th century underwent in the Shaker milieu, was due not to the individual craftsman but to the community spirit and consciousness of the Believers. It is not only a manifestation of their practicality but a witness to their common faith. Indeed one is tempted to say that it is a better, clearer, more comprehensible expression of their faith than their written theology was. The inspired Shaker simplicity, the reception of simplicity as a charismatic gift, as a sign of truth and of salvation, is powerfully and silently eloquent in the work of their hands.

These men and women, simple, profoundly serious, deeply and religiously vulnerable, open to the winds of change and grace that swept the American frontier, believed that Mother Ann, their foundress, had come from England "with the candle of the Lord in her hand" and with a definitive message. This Shaker message, which has been elaborated in strange and heterodox forms, is nevertheless in its essence deeply Christian. The United Society of Believers in Christ's Second Coming (the Shakers' official title) were not men of a dour, sulphur-and-brimstone eschatology as one might expect. They were simple, joyous, optimistic people whose joy was rooted in the fact that Christ *had* come, and that the basic Christian experience was the discovery of Christ living in us all now: so that the true Christian is the one who lives and behaves as a "Child of the Resurrection" with his eyes open to a wholly new vision of a redeemed cosmos in which war, hatred, tyranny, and greed had no place—a cosmos of creativity and worship.

In this essentially "monastic" view of life, the duty of the Believer is, as Mother Ann declared, "to labor to make the way of God your own; let it be your inheritance, your treasure, your occupation, your daily calling." This is the first principle of Shaker craftsmanship.

The Believer worked patiently, lovingly, earnestly, until his spirit was satisfied that the work was "just right." Fidelity to the demands of the workman-like conscience was a fundamental act of worship. Through this fidelity, the workman became an instrument of God's loving care for the community. His work was therefore compounded of faith and love and care. It was an expression and fruit of the Shaker covenant. In work, as in worship and in his religious dancing, the Shaker was attuned to the music intoned in each being by God the Creator and by the Lord Jesus.

Work was to be perfect, and a certain relative perfection was by all means within reach: the thing made had to be precisely what it was supposed to be. It had, so to speak, to fulfill its own vocation. The Shaker cabinetmaker enabled wood to respond to the "call" to become a chest, a table, a chair, a desk. "All things ought to be made according to their order and use," said Joseph Meacham. The work of the craftsman's hands had to be an embodiment of "form." The form had to be an expression of spiritual force. The force sprang directly from the mystery of God through Christ in the Believing artist: the "fourfold vision" of Blake is the key to the religious mystery and luminosity of Shaker craftsmanship. There were of course rules to be obeyed and principles by which the work was guided: but the work itself was free, spontaneous, itself responding to a new and unique situation. Nothing was done by rote or by slavish imitation. The workman also had a vocation: he had to respond to the call of God pointing out to him the opportunity to make a new chest of drawers like the ones that had been made before, only better. Not necessarily better in an ideal and absolute sense, but better adapted to the particular need for which it was required. Thus the craftsman began each new chair as if it were the first chair ever to be made in the world!

One can imagine, then, the Edenic innocence which is the special glory and mystery of Shaker work. Here we admire not the Titanic creativity of the self-conscious genius, aware of a possible mission to disturb and to awaken the world (and perhaps infuriated by his promethean calling). Shakers were not supposed to sign their work, or flaunt trade marks. Their only advertisement was the work itself, and the honesty with which the product was set before the buyer. Above all, the work of the Shakers was made for use rather than for profit (a maxim dear to Eric Gill). This gave it an inimitable honesty which one cannot find in the slick new model of the latest car, tailored like some unearthly reptilian fowl and flashing with pointless gadgetry, marketed to replace other models designed for obsolescence, and to be replaced itself without delay!

The Shaker had his eye not on the market but on the reality of things and on the integrity of life and thought. A Shaker Elder, planting his orchard, remarked: "A tree has its wants and wishes and a man should study them as a teacher watches a child to see what it can do. If you love a plant, take heed to what it likes. You will be repaid by it."

The Shaker's reward was in the response of living beings to his own loving care. The odd Shaker dogma about Christ "reincarnated as a woman" was perhaps not as outlandish in its original meaning as it later came to be. The root idea is that of the "maternal" aspect of God's love, and man's, an aspect too often ignored: the view which sees love as tenderness and care for all living beings (compare the Buddhist meditation on the "four unlimiteds") and indeed for life itself. Such love is one of the deepest forms of respect for the creative tenderness of God whose merciful Spirit of Love broods over all beings.

A Shaker of our own time (there are still two Shaker villages left, one in Maine and one in New Hampshire) has said: "The greatest force in the universe is the love of God . . . and the second greatest is interior prayer." One feels that for the Shaker craftsmen, love of God and love of truth in one's own work came to the same thing, and that work itself was a prayer, a communion with the inmost spiritual reality of things and so with God, not as if the "spirit" of the thing were something distinct from the thing itself, but in a full realization that everything that is, is in a certain sense "spirit," since "spirit," "form," and "actualization" are all one and the same. The Shakers thus had a deeply existential approach to reality.

It has been remarked, and it is worth repeating, that the Shaker vision was peculiarly and authentically American. This is of course a dangerously vague statement, because though there is indeed a very real and very powerful American mystique, it is becoming increasingly difficult to say precisely what it is, since every possible contradiction seems to get included in it (one need only mention the bewilderingly different expressions of freedom and unfreedom which now outdo one another in their claims to be "American"). The Shakers certainly had no political ideology. But they had a well-defined communal organization of their own, based on their religious principles. Unquestionably they felt themselves called to be a force for social renewal in the world which surrounded them. They had the gift to express much that is best in the American spirit. They exemplified the simplicity, the practicality, the earnestness, and the hope that have been associated with the United States. They exemplified these qualities in a mode of humility and dedication which one seeks in vain today in the hubris and exasperation of our country with its enormous power! Mother Ann had a beautiful and Blake-like vision of America, a vision of gentleness and love:

> I saw a large tree, every leaf of which shone with a brightness
> as made it appear like a burning torch . . . I knew that God
> had a chosen people in America; I saw some of them in vision,
> and when I met with them in America I knew them.

As Lope de Vega had said earlier (in a different context!): "There is love in the Indies—much more than here!"

Later, some of the Shaker visionaries, the "sensitives" who received inspired subjects for paintings and musical compositions, delighted in painting the "paradise tree." It was of course a peculiarly intense expression of the common hope that in America the earthly paradise had been rediscovered—certainly an essential element in the American mystique. It is interesting to note that in the legendary voyage of the Irish monk St. Brendan (6th century) the Paradise Tree of the New World plays an important and symbolic part. I think, by the way, that this particular symbolic hope needs to be taken seriously precisely in the moment of darkness and deception when, in our atmosphere of crisis, bitterness, and confusion, this hope has turned for so many into angry despair and the sacred tree has been stripped of those bright leaves and golden fruits.

Whatever may be the ambiguities and complexities of the American mystique today, let us recall the original American vocation to be a New World of almost infinite hope, a paradise of refuge, security, peace, growth, and productivity opening its arms to welcome the oppressed, the downtrodden of the "old world." Here especially the religious reformer and the idealist could find a way of realizing hitherto unrealizable hopes. Here utopias could be brought into being and here the Kingdom of God could become an earthly reality. Here the happy citizen, cultivating the rich soil, could live in an innocence and honest joy never to be troubled by intrigues and by the threat of police tyranny, as in the decadent monarchies of Europe. Here were no religious inquisitions. The American was a new being who had nothing to do with the world of European complexity and iniquity. He had only to retain his innocence and keep his "baptismal" robe unsmirched by the dark concerns of Europe the unredeemed.

The Shakers acted out their American conviction within the framework of their own order, well aware that the "world" was very much present around them, and that the serpent had come into paradise. Already the irresponsible waste of mine and forest, of water and land, the destruction of bison and elk, were there to show that Paradise was not indefinitely self-sustaining. Later the doors of the country closed to the immigrant and the refugee. American money became the greatest power in the world, and Paradise realized itself to be surrounded no longer with friendly hope but by impotent environs and frustrated hate.

Unlike Ann Lee's America, ours is, alas, without angels—perhaps because it is also seemingly without devils. Mother Ann was convinced of the reality of both. She saw the devil and fought with him, and knew he was "a real being, real as a bear." The peculiar grace of a Shaker chair is due to the fact that it was made by someone capable of believing that an angel might come and sit on it. Indeed the Shakers believed their furniture was designed by angels—and Blake believed his ideas for poems and engraving came from heavenly spirits.

This is another way of saying, with Blake, that the creative and religious imagination plays an extremely important part in the life of man, and that an era in which this spiritual imagination is impotent, sterile, or dead, is necessarily going to be an era of violence, chaos, destruction, madness, and slaughter. Describing his own picture of the Last Judgement, Blake wrote:

> When imagination, art and science and all intellectual gifts, all gifts of the Holy Ghost are looked upon as of no use, and only contention remains to man, then the Last Judgement begins and its vision is seen by the imaginative eye of everyone according to the situation he holds.

"Imagination," for Blake, is the faculty by which man penetrates ultimate reality and religious mystery. It is completely distinct from "allegorical fantasy."

"I know that this world is a world of imagination and vision (wrote Blake in a letter) . . . but everybody does not see alike. To the eyes of a miser a guinea is more beautiful than the sun, and a bag worn with the use of money has more beautiful proportions than a vine filled with grapes. The tree which moves some to tears of joy is in the eyes of others only a green thing that stands in the way. Some see nature all ridicule and deformity, and by these I shall not regulate my proportions, and some scarce see nature at all. But to the eyes of the man of imagination, nature is imagination itself. As a man is, so he sees. As the eye is formed, so are its powers. . . . To me this world is all one continuous vision of fancy or imagination."

> Why is the Bible more entertaining and instructive than any
> other book? Is it not because they [*sic*] are addressed to the
> imagination, which is spiritual sensation, and but mediately
> to the understanding or reason?

Blake's ideas of creative imagination as a necessary medium between man and the reality around him sounds less mad than it used to,
since modern science itself (so remote from Blake) has brought us face
to face with the fact that the physical constituents of the world around
us escape our understanding.

For Blake, as for the Shakers, creative imagination and religious
vision were not merely static and contemplative. They were active and
dynamic, and imaginative power that did not express itself in creative
work could become highly dangerous. So Blake could say,

> I know of no other Christianity and no other Gospel than the
> liberty both of body and mind to exercise the divine arts of
> imagination, the real and eternal world of which this vegetable
> universe is but a faint shadow and in which we shall all live in
> our eternal imaginative bodies when these vegetable bodies
> are no more. . . . What is the life of man but art and science?
> . . . Let every Christian as much as in him lies engage him-
> self openly and publically before the world in some mental
> pursuit for the building up of Jerusalem. A poet, a painter, a
> musician, an architect: the man or woman who is not one of
> these is not a Christian. . . . The unproductive man is not a
> Christian, still less the destroyer.

And finally this profoundly just and prophetic view of man's modern
plight:

> Art degraded, imagination denied, war governed the nations.

The whole history of Shaker craftsmanship and the evidence that
has been left to us in the works photographed here cry "Amen" to this
doctrine of Blake's. The chastity, the simplicity, the honesty of Shaker
work is often praised. Let these pages be a testimony to the unequalled
creative imagination of Shaker craftsmanship, which is all the greater
because it is never conscious of itself, never seeks recognition, and is
completely absorbed in the work to be done.

Shaker craftsmanship is perhaps the last great expression of work in a purely human measure, a witness to the ancient, primitive, perfect totality of man before the final victory of machine technology. A book about such craftsmanship, such wholeness, is inevitably a book with a message. It poses a challenging question: is such a spirit, such work, possible to men whose lives are in full technological, sociological, and spiritual upheaval? Will such a spirit be possible in the future world that will emerge from the present technological revolution, that world whose outlines can barely be discerned? Is Shaker craftsmanship and its spirit necessarily bound up with a more primitive technology, or can it find a way to direct and inform machine production? It is not my business to attempt an answer to a question which, in some ears, would be all but sacrilegious. It is sufficient to add my voice to those who have spoken in this book, with such sincerity and such power of persuasion.

CONTENTS

INTRODUCTION   vii
    BY THOMAS MERTON

FOREWORD   xix

PURE AND SIMPLE   3
    THE SPIRIT OF SHAKER CRAFTSMANSHIP

THE FORCES BEHIND THE FORMS   11

SPIRITUAL FUNCTIONALISM IN SHAKER FURNITURE   15
    BY ALAN GOWANS

THE PLATES
    SINGLE PIECES   21
    FURNITURE IN SHAKER SETTINGS   38
    FURNITURE IN MUSEUM SETTINGS   53
    FURNITURE IN DOMESTIC SETTINGS   78
    WESTERN SHAKER FURNITURE   93

A NOTE ON SHAKER CRAFTSMEN   102

SUGGESTED READING   105

FOREWORD

Appreciation of the quiet integrity and beauty of Shaker furniture has come about, both here and abroad, in the relatively short span of thirty-five years. Though it had been made in Shaker villages for nearly a century and a half, virtually nothing was known about the subject until 1928. In that year the first of a series of articles on the craftsmanship of the sect appeared in the magazine *Antiques*. In the 1930's, following an exhibit at the Whitney Museum of American Art, the federal government, in its art project and the culminating *Index of American Design,* devoted considerable attention to various aspects of Shaker workmanship. Interest was further increased by the publication, in 1937, of our book *Shaker Furniture: the Craftsmanship of an American Communal Sect,* and its subsequent reprintings. Other exhibits and articles have served to give this indigenous art an ever-widening recognition.

Before there was any research on Shaker architecture and handicraft, one pioneer undertaking in the field of preservation has been made in the little town of Harvard, Massachusetts, the site of one of the earliest communities. In 1920 Clara Endicott Sears began her important work of restoring and furnishing an old dwelling which had been moved from the Harvard settlement to a new site on Prospect Hill. Though the Shaker House, with its neighboring museums, Alcott's Fruitlands and the American Indian Museum, was an auspicious beginning, interest in Shaker history was relatively dormant until interpretive studies broadened knowledge of the subject. As a result of a growing literature and exhibitions in city museums, a number of projects have now been inaugurated designed to preserve what is left of the art and craftsmanship of the Believers. Besides the one at Harvard, four regional museums—at Old Chatham, New York; Hancock, Massachusetts; Pleasant Hill, Kentucky; and Auburn, Kentucky—have been organized to preserve and exhibit furniture and other artifacts. The objective at Hancock is to restore the central Church family of this lovely "City of Peace." Shaker rooms have been installed with unusual perception at the Henry Francis du Pont Winterthur Museum at Winterthur, Delaware, and the

American Museum in Britain at Claverton Manor, Bath. There are
exhibits at The Golden Lamb Inn and the Warren County Historical
Society in Lebanon, Ohio; the Western Reserve Historical Society and
the Dunham Tavern Museum in Cleveland; the Nineteenth Century
gallery at the Henry Ford Museum; Shelburne Museum, Shelburne,
Vermont; Wiggins Tavern, Northampton, Massachusetts; the Smithsonian Institution in Washington, D.C.; and the Museum of Fine Arts,
Boston, Massachusetts. A large collection of furniture, industrial materials, etc., is owned by the New York State Museum in Albany. There
are exhibits in the meetinghouses of the two remaining Shaker communities at Canterbury, New Hampshire, and Sabbathday Lake, Maine.
Several collections are still in private hands.

Our own interest has been sustained over the years. Many examples
from the productive period of Shaker craftsmanship (1790-1860), not
illustrated in our first book, have been acquired or come to our notice.
The furniture of the western societies, in Ohio and Kentucky, is now
receiving more than passing attention. Finally, our knowledge and com-
prehension have grown with experience and contacts with scholarship
in the general field. One factor, however, has remained constant: our
conviction that the distinct quality of the workmanship of the Believers
was, in essence, the result of spiritual forces, principles strictly adhered
to, and a whole-hearted commitment to a cause. As we noted earlier,
"the relationship between a way of life and a way of work" invests the
study with special meaning.

This emphasis on the spiritual or associative significance of Shaker
craftsmanship prompts us to amplify one statement in our first book.
We believed then that the furniture "can be produced again, never as
the inevitable expression of time and circumstance, yet still as something to satisfy the mind which is surfeited with over-ornamentation and
mere display." In reviewing the book, Ananda Coomaraswamy took
exception to the statement, arguing "that things are only beautiful in the
environment for which they were designed, or as the Shakers expressed
it, when 'adapted to condition.' " We would agree that, at best, a repro-
duction is only a substitute for the original, an imitation. However, if
the craftsmanship is skillful and *the craftsman in tune with the Shaker
spirit,* there is beauty and great satisfaction in the result. He is projecting
into the present the inspiration of the past.

The photographs in the present book are arranged in five categories: (a) single examples of craftsmanship, (b) furniture in Shaker settings, (c) museum installations, (d) furniture in domestic settings, and (e) examples of Ohio and Kentucky joinery. Descriptive notes provide documentation of the plates. The two essays, "Pure and Simple" and "The Forces Behind the Forms," are supplemented by an article by the art historian, Alan Gowans, of the State University of Delaware, first published in 1960 in *Dansk Kunsthaandvaerk,* the periodical of The Danish Society of Arts and Crafts and Industrial Design.

To those individual collectors and directors of institutions who have provided prints for the book we are greatly indebted. Over the years a sort of comradery has developed in this special field of American culture. Not the least of the rewards of our work is the knowledge that others, the friends we have made, have also come to care deeply for the heritage of the Shaker faith.

E.D.A.

F.A.

RELIGION IN WOOD

CHAPTER ONE

PURE AND SIMPLE

THE SPIRIT OF SHAKER CRAFTSMANSHIP

The first leaders of the Society may be compared to people going into a new country, and settling in the wilderness, where the first object is to cut and clear the land, and burn the rubbish, before the ground can be suitably prepared for cultivation. . . . But when the land is sufficiently cleared, and the (useless) rubbish consumed, and the wild vermin have all retreated, and the careful husbandman has securely fenced his field, he can then go on to prepare and cultivate his ground in peace . . . so that in a few years, this once dreary wilderness will be seen to "blossom as the rose."[1]

In the view of Seth Y. Wells and Calvin Green, the authors of the above quotation, the Shaker experiment in communitarianism was a pioneer adventure into a new country of the spirit. The Believers had left behind them the world of generation, private property, politics, and war. They sought to establish a completely new society free from the dogmas of religious "professors" and those anti-Christian influences which they felt were corrupting the life of the time. They would start afresh, choose a part of the world's wilderness for their own, clear it of "noxious vermin" and then cultivate it in peace. Their model was the primitive Christian church. The Christ spirit had come a second time, in the person of their foundress, Mother Ann Lee. For them, the long-awaited millennium was already here.

As dissenters and separatists they *had* to begin anew. In their craftsmanship, as in other aspects of their life and work, they sought such new forms of expression as would best answer their aspirations. Though they found that they could not break away entirely from the world, it is still true that to comprehend rightly the distinctive quality of their craft one must see it in the context of their beliefs, and as an integral part of the whole configuration of their culture. We must know the forces from which the forms evolved.

An early influence on Shaker doctrine and practice was that of the

3

Quakers. The Believers paid tribute to many so-called "heretical" sects, the Manicheans, Montanists, Cathari, Albigenses, Donatists, Waldenses, Anabaptists, and others, but particularly to the Quakers in the time of George Fox, whom they regarded as true witnesses of God. It was a society of Friends, under the leadership of James Wardley, a tailor of Bolton, England, and his wife Jane, which the twenty-two-year-old Ann Lee joined in 1758. Though the Wardley sect had been affected by the preaching of the French Prophets or Camisards—some of whom had found refuge in England after the revocation of the Edict of Nantes—the Quaker influence persisted in many aspects of Shaker life. Thus, in time of worship, the Believers, like their predecessors, sat quietly until the spirit moved them to speak. Both sects believed in immediate revelation, in the divine or Inner Light, in regeneration. Both bore testimony against war, oaths, slavery, . . . "vain fashions, corrupting amusements and flattering titles." Shaker simplicity of speech, with its "yea" and "nay," derived from the Friends. In fact, so similar in some respects were the two faiths that in this country Ann Lee's followers were at first called "Shaking Quakers."

More direct, however, was the influence of Ann Lee, a toiler in the textile mills of Manchester, whose testimonies regarding the nature of sin, salvation, and the millenium were the foundation of Shaker doctrine. In prison on charges of breaching the peace, she proclaimed that she had been divinely commissioned, as the manifestation of the Christ spirit in His second appearing, to fulfill the work that Jesus had begun, a work which involved repudiation of marriage and all "lusts of the flesh." Concupiscence was the cardinal sin, the bar to salvation, the source of the world's wrongs. Her mission was to regenerate mankind through the medium of a "resurrection order." After her release from prison she supplanted the Wardleys as leader of a new dispensation.

The movement thus started in England gradually took form as an organized religious society. Mother Ann, with seven followers, came to America in 1774, and two years later settled at a place called Niskeyuna (Watervliet), near Albany, New York. Profiting from revivals among the New Light Baptists in New Lebanon, New York, and adjacent towns, the Shakers actively proselyted among this and other separatist sects, and in 1781-83 extended their mission into parts of southern New England. When Ann Lee died in 1784, the foundation had been laid for eleven communities in eastern New York, Connecticut, Massachusetts, Maine, and New Hampshire. After the turn of the century the movement spread westward, where seven more colonies, in Kentucky, Ohio, and Indiana, were added to the United Society.

In a Puritan region, and at a time when the colonies were in revolt against Britain, these English-born immigrants, with their convictions on celibacy, pacifism, etc., were subject to both religious and political distrust. Persecution united them, making them aware that if their church were to survive it would have to have a strong temporal foundation. The decision to organize into monastic-like communities was justified, in their minds, by the practice of the apostolic church, where "all that believed were together, and sold their possessions, and distributed them as each had need." Private property, they held, was one of the basic causes of dissension between individuals and wars between nations. And since, in their view, that institution was indissolubly linked with marriage, they believed (unlike the Quakers) that only by separating themselves from "the course of the world" could they realize their ideal of Christian perfection.

This principle (of separation) is germane to our theme. For "the idea that the millennium had already begun freed him [the Shaker] from tradition and authority, allowing him to turn his attention in most aspects to his milieu and to approach his environment with an unforced confidence in its practical perfection."[2] In Shaker thought, laboring for perfection was an all-embracing discipline, extending to every aspect of life. "Labor to make the way of God your own," Mother Ann exhorted, "let it be your occupation, your daily calling." And again: "Do your work as though you had a thousand years to live, and as if you were to die tomorrow."

Just as Mother Ann's convictions on concupiscence were undoubtedly, in part, the result of an unhappy marital experience—she was married against her will to a Manchester blacksmith, Abraham Standerin, by whom she had four children, all of whom died in infancy—so her injunctions on such matters as cleanliness, good economy, and charity to the poor doubtless had their basis in the sordid conditions under which she lived on Toad Lane in the slums of Manchester. This was one of the narrow dirty streets, near the mills, lined with "wretched, damp, filthy cottages" in which, according to one observer, "only a physically degenerate race, robbed of all humanity, degraded, reduced morally and physically to bestiality, could feel . . . at home."[3] Ann Lee's militant spirit revolted against such squalor, and against a Church which seemed to her to do nothing to alleviate poverty and distress. She had a vision, apocalyptic in its sweep, of a better society, a community of saints aspiring to purity and perfection.

Against such an environmental background one can understand better her veritable passion for cleanliness, neatness, and order. Injunctions on such matters abound. Thus, in one testimony, Lucy Bishop (an early convert) recalled that when she was scrubbing the floor of a room, Mother Ann came in and said, "Clean your room well; for good spirits will not live where there is dirt. There is no dirt in heaven." On another occasion she addressed some sisters who had been washing the floor: "You ought to be neat, and clean, for there are no slovens nor sluts in heaven." "Provide places for your things," she told a group of Believers, "so that you may know where to find them at any time, by day or by night, and learn to be neat and clean, prudent and saving, and see that nothing is lost." At Petersham, Massachusetts, she once admonished the heads of families against "some of their costly and extravagant furniture," saying, "Never put on silver spoons, nor table cloths for me; but let your table be clean enough to eat from without cloths, and if you do not know what to do with them, give them to the poor." "Go home and put your hands to work, and your hearts to God," she told another group, "for if you are not faithful in the unrighteous mammon, how can you expect the true riches?"

Though Ann Lee and her English disciple, James Whittaker (1751-87), had formulated, in general terms, the guiding principles of the order, the chief architect of Shaker communitarianism was Joseph Meacham, formerly a lay preacher of the Baptist church in Enfield, Connecticut, who, as Mother Ann's "first born son in America," succeeded to the leadership of the society. This remarkable man survived Whittaker by only nine years, but in that time he formulated and put into operation principles of church law and government which had a profound influence on Shaker practice. His "way-marks,"[4] written sometime between 1791 and 1796, include such matters as "the order of appointment in the ministry," the duties of elders, trustees, and deacons, the importance of union and of "equal rights and privileges," the education of youth and children, instruction to the "elderly people," "instructions relative to military requisitions," and "the duty of Believers in relation to the world of mankind." Of particular interest, in connection with our present theme, are his injunctions to the deacons on standards of workmanship. On this subject he wrote:

> All work done, or things made in the Church for their own use ought to be faithfully and well done, but plain and without superfluity. All things ought to be made according to their order and use; and all things kept decent and in good order according to their order and use. All things made for sale ought to be well done, and suitable for their use.
>
> (On buildings) All work in the Church ought to be done . . . according to the order and use of things, neither too high or too low. . . .
>
> (On wearing apparel) All ought to dress in plain and modest apparel, but clean and decent according to their order and calling . . . neither too high nor too low, but in a just and temperate medium, suitable for an example to others.
>
> We are not called to . . . be like the world; but to excel them in order, union and peace, and in good works—works that are truly virtuous and useful to man, in this life.
>
> We have a right to improve the inventions of man, so far as is useful and necessary, but not to vain glory, or anything superfluous.

Meacham's way-marks influenced the Shaker covenant, and later the Millennial Laws (1823-45) which, like the Rule of Saint Benedict, regulated the temporal as well as the spiritual affairs of the community. "To each act and step," it was said of this leader, "he joined a thought of its use." The way to salvation, to perfection, was through *order* and good *use,* terms which appear over and over again in his writings. "We believed we were debtors to God in relation to Each other, and all men," the first covenant (1795) reads, "to improve our time and Tallents in this Life, in that manner in which we might be most useful." The Millennial Laws prescribe in detail not only the rights and duties of members, the order of worship, the order of the day's labor, orders concerning clothing, language, "intercourse with the world," the schooling of children, etc., but also such matters as the quality of work, the right use of

7

property, the furniture to be used in retiring rooms, and "building, painting, varnishing and the manufacture of articles for sale." In the section, "Concerning superfluities not owned," is the injunction that "Believers may not in any case or circumstance, manufacture for sale, any article or articles, which are superfluously wrought, and which would have a tendency to feed the pride and vanity of man. . . . Fancy articles of any kind, or articles which are superfluously finished, trimmed or ornamented, are not suitable for Believers." In another section, "Concerning marking tools and conveniences," the statutes forbade any craftsman to "write or print his name on any article of manufacture, that others may hereafter know the work of his hands."[5]

In the Shaker mind simplicity was the touchstone of good use. In the *Summary View of the Millennial Church* Green and Wells number it among the twelve Christian virtues, a virtue which produces thoughts, words, and works which are "wholly directed to the honor and glory of God. . . . It is without ostentation, parade, or any vain show, and naturally leads to plainness in all things."[6] But plainness was not a negative concept, except in its implication that things should be devoid of embellishment. Emphasis was on positive function: in seeking order, good use, perfection, the Shakers felt that superfluous elements, whether in dress, joinery, or building, not only obscured design and wasted time and material, but more importantly, contributed nothing to the use for which the thing manufactured was intended. "Any thing may, with strict propriety, be called perfect," Green and Wells argued, "which perfectly answers the purpose for which it was designed."

Such was the Shakers' concept of "art" or "beauty," terms they themselves seldom used. They would have preferred the medieval definition, that all art or artifacts (things made by art) were for "good use." "That which has in itself the highest use," they contended, "possesses the greatest beauty." Whether applied to "noble" ends, as in the construction and furnishing of a meetinghouse, or to "common" purposes, as in the equipment and products of shops, workmanship should be "free from error." As the late Charles Sheeler and others have noted, "they recognized no justifiable difference to be made in the quality of workmanship of any object."[7] As in the medieval guilds care was taken that no product which was imperfect in any way should be sold to the world. The Shaker order reverted to the apprenticeship system under which boys and girls indentured to the society were introduced to "the art and mystery" of the trade for which they showed preference or aptitude.

This exalted concept of use—the simplest, the most perfect fashioning of material—found expression in what Walter Gropius, writing on traditional Japanese architecture, called a "common form language." The forces which, directly or indirectly, influenced Shaker craftsmanship, evolved into a recognizable style as definite as that of any other school, Chippendale say, or Victorian, Federal, Pennsylvania Dutch. Yet the cult of simplicity never "descended to rigid forms."[8] It is hardly possible, for example, to find two sewing cabinets, or two trestle tables alike. There was freedom, within the limits of principle, to create new designs, a fact demonstrated not only in joinery but more dramatically in the field of architecture, with such achievements as the round stone barn at Hancock, Massachusetts, and the barrel-roofed meetinghouse at New Lebanon, New York. An important element in this freedom was the inspiration to excel the world in good works, "to improve the inventions of man," to do their work as though they "had a thousand years to live." Their solidly built dwellings and meetinghouses, the drawers, cupboards, and cooking arches built into interior structure, the great stone barns and mills are symbols of strength, the will to remain. Quietly the work went on, but with an inner dynamism.

Nor were there any illusions that perfection was "a state in which there [could] be no increase for the better."[9] The story is told that in her youth Mary Antoinette Doolittle, later an eldress at New Lebanon, was troubled by the meaning of "Christian perfection." In explaining it as a condition in which growth was possible, her "caretakers" compared it to a hill of corn: "When the blade first appeared, it might be perfect in that state; but it was not the ultimate. 'First the blade, then the stalk, the ear, and the full corn in the ear.'"

The flowering or "generative" period which Wells and Green predicted—a period when the wilderness would "blossom like the rose"—was a time when Shaker talent found its purest, simplest expression. Though the "gift to be simple" was, in the end, too hard to sustain, a craftsmanship which approached perfection of form during the first five or six decades of the nineteenth century testifies to an unusual spiritual afflatus. It remains as a precious part of our national heritage.

9

NOTES

1. *A Summary View of the Millennial Church* (Albany, 1823), p. 12.

2. John M. Anderson. "Force and Form: the Shaker intuition of simplicity," *Journal of Religion;* 30 (1950).

3. Frederick Engels. *The Condition of the Working Class in England in 1844* (London, 1936), p.63. Though Engels was describing a situation after the introduction of machines into the factories, living conditions could not have been much different in Ann Lee's day.

4. "A collection of the Writings of Father Joseph Meacham, Respecting Church Order and government; Evidently intended for Way-marks, for all who were or should be called in spiritual or temporal care, In the church," Rufus Bishop (comp.), New Lebanon, 1850. MS.

5. Cf. Chapter LVII, "Of the Artificers of the Monastery": "Let such craftsmen as be in the monastery ply their trade in all lowliness of mind." (*The Rule of Saint Benedict,* Translated with an introduction by Cardinal Gasquet. [London, 1925], pp.97-98.) Many parallels exist in the two rules. Thus, in Shaker practice, a person could be "shifted from his handicraft" or office if there was evidence of unseemly pride. In both communities, no gifts could be received without the abbot's (elder's) permission; abbots (elders) were subject to the provisions of both rules and shared the common life; "backsliders," if received again into the community, were relegated "to the lowest place." On journeys, Benedictine monks were to say the Divine Office wherever they are working, "kneeling in the fear of God"; similarly, the Shaker brethren, "who go out among the world, should observe . . . the order of kneeling, and should also kneel in prayer twice each day. . . ." And on their return, in both cases it was against order to "relate to another what he shall have seen or heard outside the monastery." (*Rule of Saint Benedict,* LXVII; *Millennial Laws,* Part I, Section LV, Part II, Section XV.) Anything beyond a basic assignment of clothing was considered "superfluous" in both orders.

6. *A Summary View of the Millennial Church,* p.249.

7. Constance Rourke. *Charles Sheeler, Artist in the American Tradition* (New York, 1938), p.134.

8. Charles Lane. *A Day with the Shakers* (1843).

9. *A Summary View of the Millennial Church,* p.320.

CHAPTER TWO

THE FORCES BEHIND THE FORMS

Though the Shakers are sometimes thought of as a separatist sect—separatist in the sense that they were removed from the main currents of American life—yet in striving to purify their church they were in fact within the tradition of the Pilgrims, the Puritans, the Quakers, the Baptists, and other denominations in colonial America. The Shakers went even further in this search for purification. For they wanted to make their church a society, and their society a church. After it was organized, in the late eighteenth century, it became indeed a small, integrated social order within the Great Society, its constitution or covenant based on the ethics of the New Testament. In their theology they were Millennialists and Messianists. In this theology, as well as in their economy, they also followed a communitarian ideal. Salvation was not so much an individual affair as it was a social or communal one. "The work of regeneration," wrote Benjamin Youngs, the author of the so-called Shaker "bible," "respecteth souls in a *united* capacity—in a church relation." "All that believed were together. . . ."

The Shaker movement is thus significant in that it represented a bridge, as it were, between the teachings of Jesus and the Reformation on the one hand, and social reform or secular socialism in the United States on the other. As time went on, the Shakers, as gradualists, became more concerned with reform, in their own as in the Great Society, than with purely theological matters. An experimental community such as theirs could serve, they came to believe, as a lever to exert on society at large needed reform and change. Within the framework of a successful communitarian way of life they sought to infuse, on American soil, the primitive Christian tradition.

This concept of a purified social order found expression not only in doctrine, conduct, and religious ritual, but also in the work of the hands—in building, in furniture craftsmanship, in dress, in the nature and quality of all the products of industry. To create a new earth, to establish a society freed from sin and worldliness, they sought perfection in all their endeavors. The keys to the seeking were order, usefulness, simplicity. Theirs was a daily ritual characterized by respect for manual labor, good workmanship, love of the soil, and affection one for another.

Let us examine one of these traits, the "gift to be simple"—interior simplicity, which concerned the inner man, and exterior simplicity, which showed in the labor of the hands. To the true Believers, simplicity *was* a gift, a divine call to turn away from pride and power and self to a life of the spirit. At the same time they realized that such a sublimation of self must take place under mundane conditions. They were not impractical idealists, like the Brook Farmers, for instance. They knew that discipline was necessary. The celibate life itself, a cardinal principle in Shaker theology based on the belief that marriage and its concomitant, private property, tended to obscure the sense of God in the soul, required discipline over self. But even in a disciplined order, an earthly society, a frontier society, they were still free, all the more free, to express their spiritual aspirations. For they believed they lived in the millennium, in the resurrection. And in the concept of simplicity they found a way of fulfillment.

The gift was a creative force. The Shaker artificer found that the simplest things, if made without error, were not only the most useful, but also the most satisfying to his conscience. He was happy to follow the injunction of "Father" Joseph Meacham, the inspired organizer of the United Society, that "all things ought to be made according to their order and use." Inferior workmanship, superfluous turnings, applied decoration, veneers, carvings, what Ruskin called "secondary forms or ornament," were wasteful, distracting and therefore imperfect. To adapt form to function, whether in the design of a house, a table, or a tool, was always the primary aim. He would have understood Horatio Greenough's dictum that "when the essential is found, the product is complete," or Emerson's that "the line of beauty is the result of perfect economy." "In their search for the perfection of use," the late critic, Henry McBride, once wrote, "they were, after all, reaching for perfection and perfection is the supreme attribute of art."

As to any specific or conscious code of workmanship the Shaker was seldom, however, articulate. The secret of its simplicity, its artlessness, lay in the humility which characterized his labors. What he made, to use Thoreau's words, were the products of "some unconscious truthfulness and nobleness, without even a thought for the appearance."

12

Thomas Merton, the Trappist monk, puts it this way: "The Shakers remain as witnesses to the fact that only humility keeps man in communion with truth, and first of all with his own inner truth. This one must know without knowing it, as they did. For as soon as a man becomes aware of 'his truth' he lets go of it and embraces an illusion."

Simplicity and humility were two of the foundation pillars of the Millennial Church. Reduced to practice, they serve to explain the otherwise inexplicable nature of the inspirational drawings which, produced in the course of an all too brief period, allow us to see, in another art language, the true Shaker spirit. The sisters who drew and painted these remarkable pictures had no thought of display. They were never hung on Shaker walls or otherwise exhibited. The artists did not consider themselves artists, but rather as "instruments" of God's will, and therefore what they drew, in line and color, was truth, not illusion. "Heavenly gifts," a spiritual message read, "are revealed not through vessels polished by the arts and sciences, cultivated by man, but through such as are humble and dependent children who seek to know and do God's will."

Such an approach to art or craftsmanship has relevance today. For if there is to be a renaissance in creative fields there must be a search for deeper meanings, for something besides mere technical skill, something beyond self. In the Shaker case, whatever the form of expression—the making of furniture, the building of a meetinghouse, the composition of songs or symbolic dances, the cultivation of an herb or seed garden—the Believer felt he was working in God's vineyard and should do this work, as Mother Ann Lee once said, "as though you had a thousand years to live, and as if you were to die tomorrow."

We find another significance in the workmanship of the Shakers. They were of the common people, farmers, mechanics, builders, small tradesmen, the unsung folk who made up the great body of Americans in the early years of the republic. They worked in a vernacular all their own, in forms largely underived from European or the so-called cultivated tradition. Their work is thus representative of a common strain in our heritage. In the historian's search for truth about life, Sigfried Giedion wrote in his *Space, Time and Architecture,* "it will not do for him to study only the highest artistic realizations of a period. Often he can learn more about the forces that shape its life from the common

13

objects and utensils which are the undisguised products of its industries."

The craftsmanship of the Shakers was an integral part of the life and thought of a humble but consecrated folk. They did not think of the work of their hands—in building, in joinery, in industrial pursuits of every kind—as an art, something special or exclusive, but rather as the right way of sustaining their church order, the ideal of a better society. For them the machine or tool was a "servant force." It was the purpose of work which was important. This led to a *manner* of work, which in turn gave a common character—an integrity, a harmony, a subtle but identifiable quality to all the labor of their hands.

CHAPTER THREE

SPIRITUAL FUNCTIONALISM IN SHAKER FURNITURE

BY ALAN GOWANS

> Regularity is beautiful.
>
> There is great beauty in harmony.
>
> Beauty rests on utility.
>
> All beauty that has not a foundation in use, soon grows distasteful, and needs continual replacement with something new. That which has in itself the highest use possesses the greatest beauty.

Who set down principles like these? Not, as we might guess, some disciple of William Morris, some product of the Bauhaus; these are the declarations of craftsmen working in the late eighteenth and at the beginning of the nineteenth century in the colonies of "the people called Shakers." And when we look at what these craftsmen produced, the modern parallels are even more pronounced. Here is the same concern for "basic design," the same scorn for extrinsic decoration, the same emphasis on the nature of materials, that we have come to look for in sound contemporary work. Who were these people, seemingly so far ahead of their time?

The Shakers, as they were popularly known—or the United Society of Believers in Christ's Second Appearing, as they called themselves—were an evangelical sect founded in Manchester, England, in the 1770's by a religious visionary named Ann Lee. Like many other eighteenth-century groups in England, France, and Germany, they were in reaction against what they considered the worldly complacency that had overtaken established churches all over Europe after the religious wars. And like many others, too—like the German Moravians and the Ephrata society in Pennsylvania, for instance—the Shakers were drawn to America, partly in hope of escaping persecution at home, more with the expectation of founding in the wide free spaces of the New World

15

new, pure societies where they could live the Godly life without fear of contamination from an older, sinful world. Led by Ann Lee, the Shakers arrived in New York in 1774, went on up the Hudson, and established themselves in the then wild unsettled back country of New England and upstate New York. There, after a first few hard years, they made converts and soon began to prosper mightily. The first half of the nineteenth century was their heyday; by 1850 there were eighteen Shaker colonies in existence, eleven of them in New England, the others as far afield as Ohio, Indiana, and Kentucky. After the Civil War, however, what seems to be the common fate of utopias began to overtake them. From a high of some 6,000 or so in 1850 their numbers dwindled to no more than 1,000 by the end of the century; one after another their colonies became extinct, and today only two, with two dozen or so members, survive. At the same time, however, interest in their crafts—their furniture especially—began to grow steadily, until today it could almost be said that the Shaker religious cult has been replaced by an aesthetic one.

Of course there was nothing entirely unique about the Shaker movement. American history is studded with such "holy experiments," from the Puritans and Quakers of the seventeenth century to the Owenites and Mormons in the nineteenth. A number of these, like the Shakers, emphasized celibacy; most of them laid particular stress on arts and crafts as "godly work." What makes Shaker arts more distinctive than others, and of such particular interest to contemporary designers, is their unusual simplicity. For this there were two reasons. The first and (from the design point of view) less important, was the Shaker emphasis on "unworldliness": "Fancy articles of any kind . . . superfluously finished, trimmed, or ornamented, are not suitable for Believers," declared the Society's *Millennial Laws*; "Whatever is fashioned, let it be plain and simple, unembellished by superfluities which add nothing to its goodness or durability. Think not that ye can keep the laws of Zion while blending with the forms and fashions of the children of the unclean!"

But this in itself was nothing new; no monastic community in history ever set out to encourage inordinate display. What made the Shaker doctrine of plainness so unusually rigorous was that it was superimposed on what was already the powerfully plain tradition of New England. The Moravians of Pennsylvania, for instance, also encouraged simplicity, but because their craftsmen brought with them the elaborate decorative traditions of German folk art, Moravian crafts remained quite ornate despite religious strictures. Shaker craftsmen, on the other hand, came mostly of lower-middle-class New England stock; their new principles only served to reinforce an existing predisposition against "worldly ornament" inherited from the seventeenth-century Puritan world. The result was a "double-barreled" stimulus, so to speak, which produced an extreme simplicity unrivaled by the craftsmanship of any other American sect—and very pleasing to modern eyes.

But is Shaker art really proto-modern? That all depends. Certainly if we consider merely the outward forms, the simplicity, the honestly expressed construction, we could say so. And when we learn that Shaker crafts were determinedly communal, done by and for the community as a whole, we are reminded of something like the ideals of William Morris and the Bauhaus. But the similarity emphatically stops there. Not only was individual expression discouraged to the point of forbidding craftsmen to identify their own work in any personal way, but the very concept of individual inspiration was denied. "The Shakers believe," wrote a mid-nineteenth-century visitor to the Niskeyuna (Watervliet, New York) community, "that their furniture was originally designed in heaven, and that the patterns have been transmitted to them by angels." That such a theory of art has any direct historical antecedents is to say the least doubtful (Ann Lee, the foundress, could not read or write); but if it has any indirect historical connections, they lie certainly more in the direction of Plato's doctrine of archetypal forms, of the theory of absolute beauty, than of modern aesthetics.

But there is an even more fundamental difference than this. The "pioneers of modern design" (to use Pevsner's phrase) all had in common a strong awareness of historical time. By this I don't mean that they were uninterested in universal principles, valid for all time—of course they were, and terms like "The International Style" commemorate this broad outlook—but that they all worked with an eye on posterity, or "the art of the future." From at least 1850 on, an awareness of history has been endemic in Western society, and nowhere more than in the arts. Our artists think normally and instinctively in terms of "movements" and "influences"; they are consciously aware of the relationship of their work to the past, and concerned about its effect on future development. Frank Lloyd Wright, for instance, was of all contemporary figures perhaps the most independent, the most inclined to think of himself as having evolved in a vacuum, inspired only by his own genius; yet he never tired of citing his debt to "lieber Meister" Sullivan, or of complaining that he would not live long enough to "remake the face of America." Mondrian justified his painting by the claim that it could create a more peaceful and orderly environment for future generations; Kandinsky hoped he could make posterity more spiritually minded, and so on.

Now with this kind of thinking people like the Shakers had nothing in common. The Shakers, or the Mennonites, or the Moravians, were not interested in what "posterity" would think of them, in leaving memorials of their work to influence future generations. Too often, as armies swept back and forth across Germany, or as English mobs gathered to sack the homes and meeting places of "fanaticks," they had seen the labors of years—let alone of lifetimes and generations—ruined in a day, for them to put any of their treasure into years ahead. They lived for the present, and they worked for the present; as they would have put it, *Now* is the time for salvation, *now* is the acceptable year of the Lord. "Labor until ye bring your spirits to feel satisfied. . . .": that was The Holy Law of Zion. How well they did the job now, how conscientiously they worked today—whether cleaning stables or carving chairs, turning sod or binding books, raising barns or planing chests—in the sight of the Lord, now, was what counted. They lived and worked in a timeless present.

This sense of timelessness is at the root of all we think of as typical of arts like the Shakers'. It explains the characteristic lack of stylistic consciousness, for instance. Obviously, some of the late eighteenth- and early nineteenth-century Shaker converts were trained craftsmen, and knew the prevalent trends of style in, say, New England furniture; you can see it clearly in the forms of their ladder-back chairs, their architectural details, the proportions of chests, and so on. But they had no interest in perpetuating the New England tradition as such, still less in "keeping up with the times" by following the shifts and trends of taste generally between, say, 1780 and 1860. When finally in late Shaker work evidence of Victorian taste does begin to creep in, it is a telling sign of the impending collapse of the Society, of the withering of its spiritual roots. Most important, it explains the emphasis on perfection of craftsmanship.

Precisely because the Shaker craftsman was so unconcerned with the future, he produced an art of enduring merit, that posterity enjoys and admires long after more historically minded art has been discarded. This may seem a paradox; but it is a paradox that runs all through the history of art. If there is any principle at all to be deduced from the broad study of art history, it is surely this—great art, like all other intangibles, is most often the by-product of some other aspiration. In the "Golden Age of Greece," so-called, "the highest panegyric accorded to Pheidias by his contemporaries was not that he had erected works of art, but that he had enriched the received religion of the State"; it was not until the great age of creativity was over, "in the full Hellenistic age," that "the dilettante, the collector, the antiquarian made their appearance." Or again, when the great cathedrals were being built, "the medieval artist no more believed in self-conscious aesthetic canons than he believed that God had made the blossom or the songbird for no other purpose than to inspire some springtime lyrist. . . ." So wrote F. B. Chambers in *Cycles of Taste* (New York, 1932); it is possible to quibble over many supporting details of the theory he sets forth, but hardly over its general conclusion. Anybody can observe it for himself. The more consciously and deliberately you set out to "create a work of art," the more unlikely you are to produce much of lasting significance. So with the Shakers. Creating a great art, or even a distinctive cultural expression, was the last thing they had in mind. Their art—doing the best job they could on whatever their hand was set to do—was ultimately intended not to delight their own or anyone else's aesthetic sensibilities, but as an expression of their spiritual life—as an immediate means to Heaven, if you like. Consequently—and we can use the word advisedly—theirs was an enduring achievement. Consequently, too, as soon as its religious rationale began to fail, Shaker art began to fade. Once its creators became self-conscious (as they did after 1870), once they began to look at their art as art, once they began to evaluate it by the standards of this world, all at once it seemed quaint and old-fashioned at best, at worst rude and worthless. It was not celibacy but spiritual dessication, not the machine production of this world but a failing vision of the next, that destroyed Shaker culture. And in all this there is much for modern craftsmen to ponder.

THE PLATES
SINGLE PIECES

Latch, wrought iron. From Hancock, 1830.

Shoemakers candle stand. Cherry. Height 16½″. From New
Lebanon Church family, c. 1800. Authors' collection.

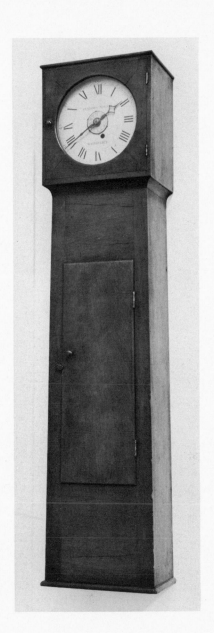

Shaker clock. Made by Benjamin Youngs, Watervliet (New York), c. 1812. Cherry case. Height 41¼″. width 9½″ (at base), depth 5¼″ (at base). Lower section tapers slightly from base to top. Brass movement with alarm attachments. Property of Western Reserve Historical Society, Cleveland, Ohio. A similar if not identical grandmother's alarm clock is in the Henry Ford Museum at Dearborn, Michigan. One of Youngs' "tall" clocks, made at "Water Vliet" about 1806, is illustrated in *Antiques* (April, 1929).

Sewing "desk." Pine and maple. Height 34″, width 27¼″, depth 21″. The slide can be pulled out for sewing or writing. From New Lebanon, c. 1840. Property of Mr. and Mrs. John D. Rockefeller, 3rd.

Swivel sewing chair or stool, with metal spokes. Height 26½″ (to top of rail), diameter of seat, 15″. From New Lebanon, c. 1835. Property of Mr. and Mrs. John D. Rockefeller, 3rd.

25

Chest of drawers. Pine. Height 39¼″, width 44″, depth 36¾″. New
Lebanon (?). Property of Mr. and Mrs. John D. Rockefeller, 3rd.

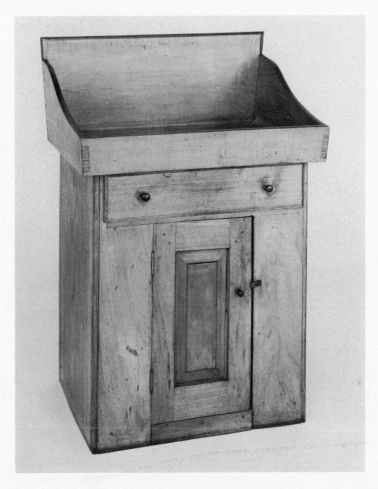

Wash stand. Pine and maple. Height 38″, length 27″, depth 21″.
From Hancock, c. 1820. Property of Mr. and Mrs. Charles Sheeler.

Elders' or trustees' desk. Pine and hickory. From Hancock or New
Lebanon. Early. Height 46¼″, width 48½″, depth 36½″. Property
of Mr. and Mrs. John D. Rockefeller, 3rd.

Two-drawer blanket chest. Pine, stained red. From
Hancock, c. 1830.

Kitchen table with splay legs and one drop leaf. From Hancock, c. 1820. The steel candlesticks were Shaker-made at New Lebanon.

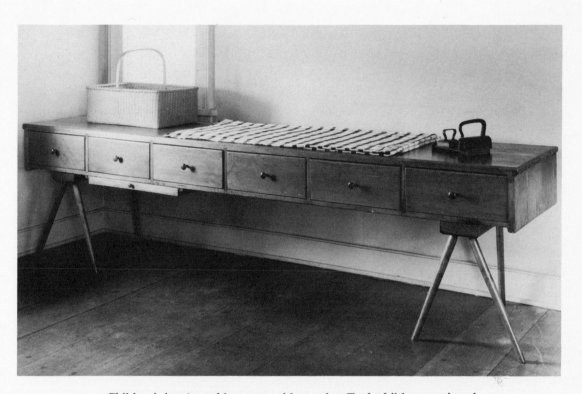

Children's ironing table on movable trestles. Each child was assigned a place and a drawer. Case is pine. From New Lebanon Church family. Property of Mr. and Mrs. John D. Rockefeller, 3rd.

Table and table desks. The table, painted red, consists of two stands joined by a one-board top. Length 55″, width 20″, height 25″. From the canning kitchen of the North family. New Lebanon. Early table desks also from New Lebanon, c. 1835. Pine. Authors' collection.

Wash bench. Pine. From New Lebanon North family, c. 1820.
Length 56½″, height 24⅞″ (36″ to top of back board), depth 15″
(at base, 17¼″ at top). The tin can was for kerosene. Sugar bucket.
Authors' collection.

Tailoresses' counter or "bench." Curly maple except for drop leaf. Four wooden casters fixed into base of frame facilitate movement of piece. Top, 72″ by 32″, height 33″. From Hancock, c. 1840. Property of Mr. and Mrs. John D. Rockefeller, 3rd.

Cupboard chest. Pine. Height 81″, width 35¾″, depth 18½″. From
Hancock, c. 1820. Property of Mr. and Mrs. Charles Sheeler.

Sill cupboard. Paneled doors and top and sill mouldings. Pine. Watervliet community, c. 1820. Height 62¾″, width 38″, depth 13″ (at top), 19″ (below sill). Pine. Authors' collection.

Shaker forms: Small pine bench from New Lebanon. Early. Side
chair, with tilting buttons. From Hancock, c. 1820 (Two views).
Armed rocking chair and candlestand. Church and Second families.
From New Lebanon.

FURNITURE IN SHAKER SETTINGS

Shaker furniture . . . may not be fully understood or appreciated except in the surroundings that it was designed to occupy. . . . The totality to which Shaker furniture contributed was one of spiritual harmony rather than decorative completeness. Or, to put it another way, each element in a Shaker room was like a single note in a simple tune and hence largely dependent for its significance upon appropriate association with other notes in a sequence keyed to the same environment. . . .

HOMER E. KEYES,
Antiques, (December, 1934).

Pegboards in meeting house, Hancock, 1786. Installed in almost every room in shops, dwellings, and churches, the peg board, or peg rack, was a veritable symbol of Shaker order and convenience. On the pegs were hung dresses and coats, bonnets and hats, household utensils and tools, mirrors, clocks, chairs—anything suspensible. The interior woodwork of meeting houses was painted a Prussian blue.

A room in the "wash house" or laundry at the New Lebanon Church order (1806). In such well-lighted rooms, with their white plastered walls, peg boards, and doors, window casings, and floors stained a warm yellow or reddish brown, there was perfect harmony between the furnishings and their architectural environment. The small windows gave light to an inner room.

Door with transom ventilator. North family, New Lebanon.

Writing desk on tripod base. Maple. Swivel chair and foot warmer (butternut). Such desks were used by the deaconesses in charge of "temporalities in the female line." Hancock community.

"There are no hiding-places for dirt or cobwebs; the speckless walls present a polished surface, unbroken by mirror or picture." (A. B. Harris, "Among the Shakers," *The Granite Monthly* [April 1877].)

Trestle table and side chairs. Ministry's dining room, Church family dwelling, Hancock, 1830–32. The Shaker ministry, consisting of two "elder brothers" and two "elder sisters," ate in a separate room adjoining the larger one used by the rest of the family.

"If one's preconceived idea about the rooms is that they are unattractive, by reason of the austerity in furnishing, and the general primness—that is altogether a mistake. There is an aesthetic, as well as a very practical side. . . . there is refreshment in the absolute cleanliness and tidiness and order. . . ." (Harris, "Among the Shakers.")

42

Built-in cupboard, soapstone heating plate, and "arch." "Nurse shop" (infirmary) at North family, New Lebanon, c. 1810. Cane was occasionally used in seating chairs, though splint (and later tape) was the usual material.

Built-in cupboard, painted blue, in anteroom of a chamber on the second floor of the Hancock meetinghouse, no longer standing. The ministry of each Shaker bishopric had their "dwelling place" in the meetinghouse and worked in a separate "ministry shop."

Stairway from first to second loft, Hancock Church family dwelling.

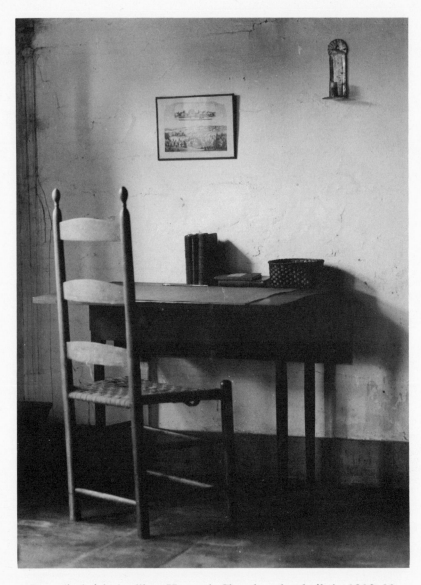

Room in brick dwelling, Hancock Church order, built in 1830–32. In this three-story building, with basement and two upper "lofts," there were 100 large doors, 245 cupboard doors and 369 built-in drawers. Rooms were heated by small wood-burning stoves of the "Shaker improvement."

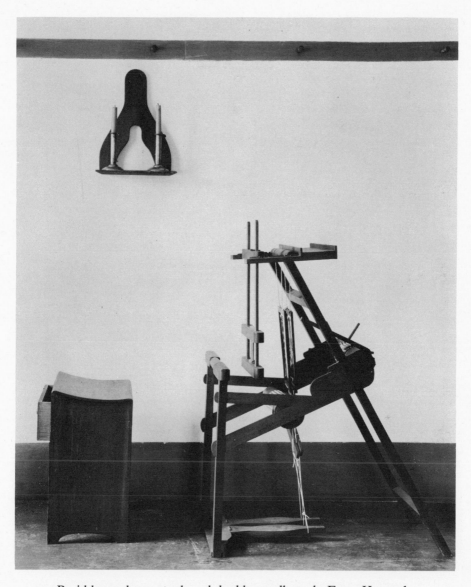

Braid loom, loom stool, and double candle rack. From Hancock.

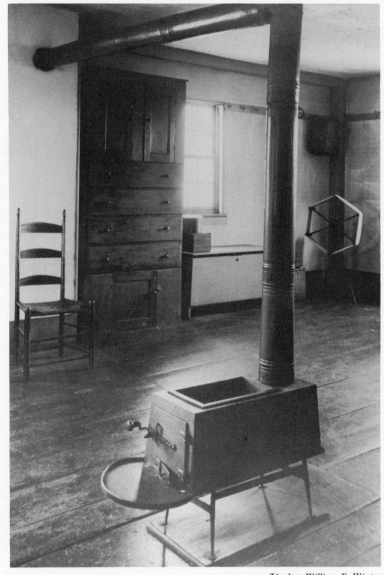

Weave room in a sisters' shop at Hancock as it appeared about 1930.
The stove has a receptacle for heating flatirons. To concentrate heat
on the irons, this was often covered by a portable tin cap which the
Shakers, for reasons unknown, called a "cappadocia."

Built-in storage drawers and cupboards in the upper loft of a North
family, New Lebanon dwelling. Pine, stained a soft brown.

Rooms no longer used often appeared like this one, in the wash-house of the First Order, New Lebanon, when the authors were making their collection of Shakeriana. The cupboards are part of the permanent architecture of the room.

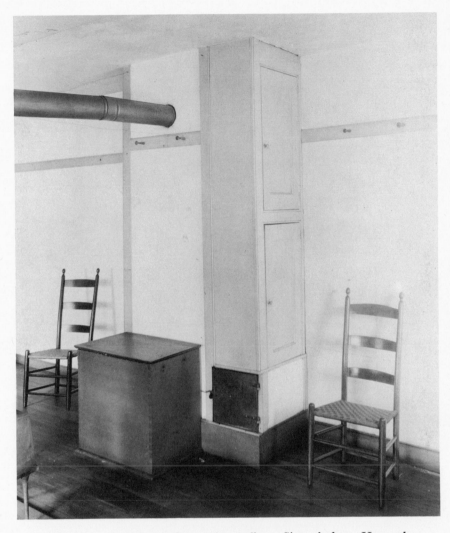

Built-in cupboards, chairs, and woodbox. Sisters' shop. Hancock.
No longer standing.

Visitors' benches, New Lebanon meeting house, 1822–24.

FURNITURE IN MUSEUM SETTINGS

Several museums devoted to the preservation of Shaker furniture have installed, or plan to install Shaker rooms or groupings. Others have had exhibitions of craftsmanship and Shaker religious arts, with careful attention to the reconstruction of the rooms in which the materials were shown. Shown in the present section are installations at the Henry Francis du Pont Winterthur Museum, the American Museum in Britain, the Philadelphia Museum of Art (in a temporary exhibition in 1962), the Shaker Museum at Old Chatham, New York, the Shaker House at the Fruitlands Museums in Harvard, the Shaker village at Hancock, the New Hampshire Historical Society, and the Smithsonian Institution.

Henry Francis du Pont Winterthur Museum

View of the main Shaker room. The rocking chair is different from most New Lebanon armchairs in having five instead of four slats. The stove is fitted with a branched prong for holding shovel and tongs. The trestle table is a Hancock type.

53

The cupboards and drawers, with their lovely original yellow ochre
stain, came from an upper loft in an early Enfield, New Hampshire,
Shaker dwelling.

Storage room from the same source. Note the shelf over the window,
which looks out into a medicinal herb shop.

Counter with drop leaf, from the sisters' shop at the South family, Watervliet, New York. Maple and pine, lightly stained. A brother's armed rocking chair, early, from Hancock. Sewing stand from the Second family, New Lebanon. Drop-leaf table with splay legs, New Lebanon. Looking glass on hanging rack. Three-step stool. The paneled window casing, painted a heavenly blue, came from the Hancock meetinghouse, which was razed in the 1930's. All pieces were formerly in the Andrews Collection.

The tall chest of drawers is from the collection of Mr. and Mrs. Charles Sheeler. Height 84″, width 37½″, depth 19″. To the left of the chest is an armed bench, with six legs. Height 28¾″, length 74¾″, depth 20½″. Lent by Mr. and Mrs. John D. Rockefeller, 3rd. To the right of the chest is a settee made at Enfield, New Hampshire, 1855–56. Height 33¼″, length 61″, depth 17″. Lent by Mr. and Mrs. Julius Zieget. Benches and three-drawer ironing table in foreground are from the Sheeler Collection. Dimensions of table: height 29¼″, length 130¼″, width 32¼″.

57

Retiring, or bedroom. Blanket chest, candle stand, and one-drawer table lent by Mr. and Mrs. Julius Zieget. The stand came from the North family at New Lebanon: height 25″, diameter of top 18″. The table is a Canterbury piece: height 27¾″, length 36″, width 21¼″. The armed rocker is a mid-nineteenth-century New Lebanon type.

Desk made at the Union Village, Ohio, community. Lent by the Warren County (Ohio) Historical Society. The slide above the drawer is an interesting feature. Height 36″, width 23″, depth 20″.

Case of drawers from the Watervliet, Ohio, community. Date and use not recorded. Height 60″, width 36″, depth 11″. Lent by Mr. and Mrs. Robert H. Jones, Lebanon, Ohio.

Low work counter with two drawers and one-board top, from the communal kitchen at Hancock. Pine. The top is 27½″ by 53″; height 27″.

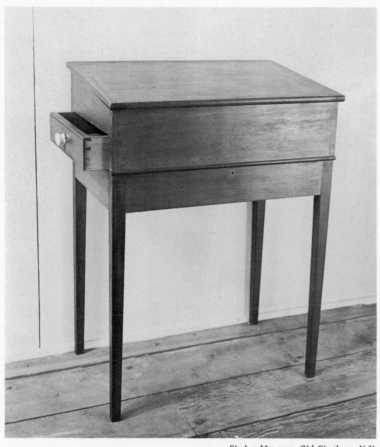

Small lift-top desk made by Abram Ellis at Watervliet. Pine with cherry legs. One drawer and a small drawer for ink pot. The top is 21¾″ by 13½″. Height ranges from 27¼″ to 28¼″.

The bent-wood chair at the right is a variant of the usual Shaker design. It is said to have been made by Gabriel Hawkins of the Second or South family, Mount (New) Lebanon, for the Philadelphia Centennial in 1876. Another variant is the spindle-back chair at the left, supposed to have been made by Robert Wagan at Mount Lebanon. When imitations of Shaker chairs were introduced into the market by several manufacturers, Wagan stamped on his chairs a gold transfer Trade Mark as a guarantee of their Shaker origin.

Shaker Museum, Old Chatham, N.Y.

A fine example of the scroll-arm rocking chair, from the Canterbury society. The table, also from Canterbury, is curly and birdseye maple. Length 33¾″, width 19″, height 25¾″. It has turned legs and one drawer.

Settee from the North family, New Lebanon. The seat is pine,
the rest ash or/and maple. Length, 68″; height of seat, 15″;
width of seat, 14″.

Solicitous care for the aged and infirm was a Shaker trait. The invalid's chair, from New Lebanon, was constructed from an early armed rocker. The walking frame, or "walker," of maple, was probably made at Enfield, New Hampshire. Height 32″.

Small pine sink with rectangular iron basin, Watervliet (?). Length 25″; width at top, 10½″; width at base, 21″; height in front, 32″; height at back, 45½″.

"Long room" in the Shaker House. The building was commenced
in 1794 and occupied in the summer of 1795 as an office, with living
quarters above. Trestle tables, chairs, and case furniture are characteristic of the craftsmanship of the Harvard and Shirley communities.

Shaker House, Fruitlands Museums, Harvard, Mass.

Kitchen exhibit in the Shaker House. Of particular interest are the armed rocking chairs, products of the chair shop at Harvard.

That chairmaking was a considerable industry at Harvard is indicated by the following entry in a Shaker journal: "Jan. 28, 1843. An account of chairs made in this family in the year 1841 and 1842, Elder Brother Thomas Hammond foreman in making chairs. Amount, including all sizes, 339. There was put at the office 83 common, 3 rocking chairs with arms, and 6 small ones—92 in all." (*Gleanings from Old Shaker Journals,* Clara Endicott Sears, comp. [Boston, 1916].)

Hancock Shaker Village

Room in brick dwelling, Hancock Church family, built in 1830-32. In this three-story building, with basement and two upper "lofts," there were 100 large doors, 245 cupboard doors, and 369 built-in drawers. Rooms were heated, as here, by small wood-burning stoves. The chair at the right is for shop or high-counter use. The drawer in the sewing stand (a Hancock piece) can be used by two sisters sitting opposite each other.

Note: Much of the furnishings of the dwelling and shops at Hancock is from the Andrews Collection, and will eventually be catalogued in pamphlet form. Many of the pieces are pictured and documented in *Shaker Furniture: The Craftsmanship of an American Communal Sect.*

69

The side chair, with cane seat, is from the Enfield, New Hampshire, Shaker colony, the armed rocking chair from Canterbury. The stove was designed for the Canterbury colony and cast in the Ford foundry, Concord, New Hampshire, in 1850. The medial-stretcher table is pine and maple. On it are oval boxes, and a tape loom from the Harvard community. Attribution of the portrait of a "Shaker" woman is doubtful.

"Furniture of the Shaker Sect" is an installation in the Hall of Everyday Life in the American Past, Museum of History and Technology. High cupboard case, small desk, sewing cabinet, and chairs. The high swivel stool is an unusual piece. Objects lent to the museum by Dr. Gerald McCue.

71

Trestle table—probably used in Ministry Dining Room; 3-drawer infirmary wash-stand, Sister's 2-drawer sewing stand, and 3-slat chair; 1 drawer blanket chest; stove. Furnishings courtesy of Dr. J.J.G. McCue.

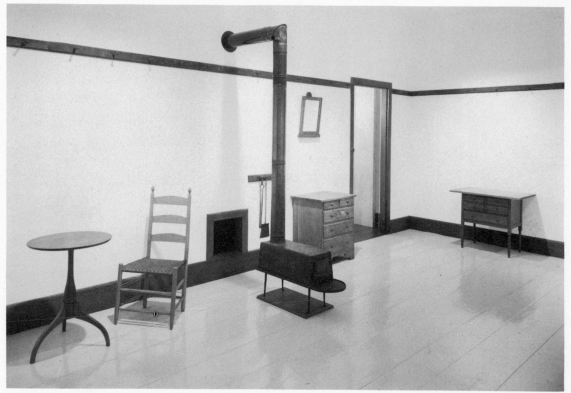

Cherry candle-stand & 3-slat chair; Stove, small chest of drawers for
sewing room; mirror and rack; Hancock sewing table. Furnishings
courtesy of Dr. J.J.G. McCue.

Trestle table for ministry use. Made of walnut and ash. Early bench;
2-slat chair on peg rack; food safe, 1830: pine with pricked tin panels
for ventilation. Used at South Union Colony.

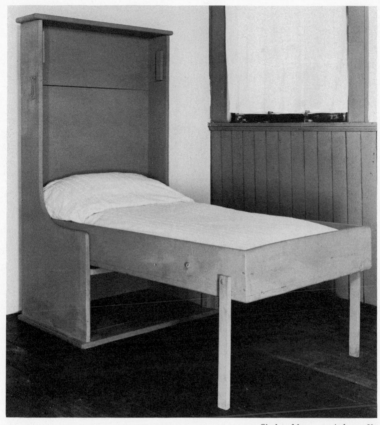

Child's folding bed. Painted Shaker blue. Bed can be folded and
locked with hook on left side when not in use. Shakertown at
Pleasant Hill, Ky. Inc.

Shakertown at Pleasant Hill, Ky., Inc.

Retiring room. Walnut table 29¾″ x 26½″, height 28″. Bed; width 33½″, length 74¼″; rocker of maple and hickory, hanging cupboard; cherry, width 27¼″, height 51¼″, 3 shelves. Towel rack, poplar and pine. Washstand: cherry. Top 18¼″ x 24¾″. Height 29″.

Shakertown at Pleasant Hill, Ky., Inc.

Dining room side table is cherry; 27½″ x 31½″, height 27½″; dining table top is poplar, legs are walnut—41½″ x 70″, height 28½″. Chairs of mixed woods, hickory, maple and poplar, painted dark red. Wood box, poplar, width 26″, depth 14½″, height at back 36″. Drawer in bottom for kindling.

FURNITURE IN DOMESTIC SETTINGS

As one Shaker community after another was dissolved, the furnishings of the dwellings and shops were auctioned off or otherwise dispersed. But with the increased interest in American antiques in the 1930's, and the awakening interest in the Shakers' furniture a decade or so later, collectors began to seek out examples of their craftsmanship, though the supply by this time was limited. There are now several homes in the country furnished, in whole or in part, with Shaker pieces.

Dining table, pine and maple. Length 168″, width 34″, height 27″. From the South family, New Lebanon. Now in the Shaker-built house of Mr. John Roberts, Canaan, New York. The Canaan Upper family, a branch of the North family in New Lebanon, was started in 1813 and fully organized by 1821. It was dissolved in 1897.

No pictures were ever hung on Shaker walls.

Built-in drawers and cupboards in the dining room of the John Roberts house. Pine. The unit is 43 inches wide and about 8 feet high, the height of the room. The drop-leaf table has square tapering legs. The house, formerly a sisters' shop, was built in 1854. John Roberts house.

"Evidently those who planned the domestic arrangements, while they had in view handiness and compactness, did not overlook the fact that there might be a great saving of noise and labor in the construction of furniture; and so, as far as practicable, they had presses and heavy benches built into the wall, instead of movable fixtures." (Harris, "Among the Shakers." Cf. plates in Furniture in Shaker Settings Section.)

Early pine cupboard-case from New Lebanon. Height 79″, width 30″, depth 18″. At the base is a hinged dust lid. John Roberts house.

Living room in the house of the late Mrs. John Spring, Gloucester, Massachusetts—an early collector of Shaker furniture. Of particular interest is the (ministry's) trestle table, with urn-shaped legs, from the Harvard or Shirley society. To the right, only partially shown, is a writing desk mounted on a standard with trestle feet. The desk can be raised or lowered to a given height by inserting a wooden pin in holes bored in the vertical member of the standard, an example of Shaker ingenuity in designing furniture for convenient use. In front of the desk is a New Lebanon-type swivel stool.

Another example of Shaker ingenuity, formerly in the Spring collection, is a combination table-desk with a long deep frame, at each end of which are two drawers set one above the other. A single drop leaf at the side can be raised by a slide to a position level with the top. Another slide, placed directly beside the first, has a slanting top so that the leaf, when up, is held at an angle convenient for writing.

A view of the sisters' shop at Tyringham, Massachusetts, now the home of Mr. and Mrs. John S. Rudd. The long table was originally used as a laundry table at the Church family or First Order, New Lebanon. It is cherry, with two drop leaves and a drawer at each end. Length 78¼", width 39¼" (with leaves up), height 27¼".

The Shakers settled in Tyringham in 1792, eventually forming two families. The community was dissolved in 1875, the remaining members moving to Hancock and Enfield, Connecticut, in the same bishopric.

The Rudds have two of these lovely Hancock washstands. Pine, with dovetailed rim, yellow stain allowing the grain to show. Width 24″, depth 16″, height (to top) 40″.

"Doorway to quietude." End of kitchen in the country home of Edward Deming and Faith Andrews, Richmond, Mass. The house is a late eighteenth-century salt box. The tin cupboard and woodbox came from the New Lebanon community. The broom is a fitting symbol of Shakerism, and broom- and brush-making one of the basic industries of the order. "The Shaker broom is always hung up against the wall when not in use."

Settee in cherry wood, from the North family Novitiate or Gathering order, New Lebanon. The rails are equipped with a series of knobs for the cording. A unique piece formerly in the Andrews Collection at "Shaker Farm" in Richmond.

Ezra Stoller

"Shaker Farm," the living room. Hardware used in the restoration is Shaker made. The tin chandelier, with cylinder for holding candles, once lighted the meeting house of the Tyringham, Massachusetts, community. The wash bench came from the North family at New Lebanon, the green blown bottles and jars (not Shaker made) from the medicinal herb shops in that community. In right foreground, an early brethren's armchair and adjustable candle rack. The stove, from the meetinghouse at Hancock, has delicately wrought legs with pad feet. At the left is a loom stool with drawer and leather seat. The carpet is similar to those woven by the Shakers.

Tom Yee

Eight foot trestle table—4 board top with maple trestles, 28¼″ width; 1-slat maple dining chairs—accompanying bench is maple and pine; tall narrow 2-door cupboard of pine was originally for small tinware. Fruit tray stained red from the canning room at Sabbathday Lake, Maine. Cobbler's candlestand with steel candlesticks. Pine mirror frame set on typical rack. Home of the late Edward Deming Andrews, and Faith Andrews, Pittsfield, Mass.

Tom Yee

Retiring room—maple and cherry sewing desk from the Harvard, Mass. Society. The front strip of the rimmed top is 36″ wide and was used as a measuring stick; 2-slat chair with ebony finish was made for "the world". The 2-step stool was a necessary item in every sewing room. Home of the late Edward Deming Andrews, and Faith Andrews, Pittsfield, Mass.

School library cupboard of pine. Door is hinged in center so that it may be left half-way open if necessary. The 2 pegs at top of cupboard are for the hanging of maps when needed. Height 7′ 11½″, width 30″, depth 15½″. Pine counter used in the print shop—has small rollers underneath to facilitate moving. Top 28¼″ width one board. Width at base 25¾″, height 33″. From the home of Mr. and Mrs. David Volk Andrews, Hastings-on-Hudson, N.Y.

Pine and maple counter originally used in Shaker workroom. The top is one board, 28¼″ width by 9′11″, height 33″. From the home of Mr. & Mrs. David Volk Andrews, Hastings-on-Hudson, N.Y.

Herb cupboard of butternut. Used in the New Lebanon, N. Y. North family infirmary. Width 47″, depth 13¼″ and 18½″, height 66″. Interior of each drawer is partitioned for the storage of herbs. Labels on each drawer tell of its contents as follows—Wormwood, Mother Wort, Cocash, Peppermint, Penny Royal, Spearmint, Lemon Balm, Catfoot, Tanzy, Boneset. From the home of Mr. & Mrs. David Volk Andrews, Hastings-on-Hudson, N.Y.

School desk of oak and cherry, early nineteenth century. The armed rocker with tape-woven seat and back was made and sold to "the world," about 1880. The candlestand is maple. "Shaker Farm," summer home of the Andrews, Richmond, Mass.

WESTERN SHAKER FURNITURE

The furniture of the Ohio and Kentucky Shakers, though marked by the same austere simplicity and fine workmanship as that of their eastern brethren, exhibits, as does their architecture, certain regional characteristics which place it in a special category. Tables, stands, chests, beds, etc., in general, are heavier in their component parts and therefore somewhat more severe in appearance than their prototypes in the East. Differences may be accounted for, in part, by the materials used. Whereas in the East pine, maple, cherry, birch, and butternut were the common woods, in the West the "timber for furniture" was chiefly poplar (whitewood) and black walnut. (Cherry, pine, and butternut were also used, but to a much less extent.) In the second place, the western craftsmen were removed, in time and space, from the traditions which came to affect furniture style in eastern New York and New England, giving it a recognizable character by the time the western communities were established. Though the work of the builders and joiners in the West was influenced by Shaker principles no less than that of the eastern artisans, and though they adopted certain forms and devices—the peg board, wooden pulls on drawers, the three-slat side chair, the sill cupboard, etc.—one feels that in the largely autonomous Ohio–Kentucky societies craft practices developed with a degree of independence. There was considerable communication and intervisitation between the leaders in the East and West, but no comparable contacts between craftsmen and builders. When Rufus Bishop and Isaac Youngs, for instance, journeyed from New Lebanon to the West in 1834, they visited Timothy Bonel's shop in Union Village, Ohio, where he made "chairs and wheels." Though "tilting chairs" had been made in the East for some time, Brother Timothy did not know of "our manner of fixing chairs with balls, etc.," and had to be informed. Another evidence of a lack, break, or lag in Shaker craft tradition is the superfluous turnings one sometimes finds on the legs of western desks, tables, and stands. Such superfluities, a sign of creeping worldliness, occurred, to be sure, in late eastern styles, but at a later period than in the West. Though it is difficult to account specifically for such regional diversity,

93

one must remember that the western communities, especially those in Kentucky, were peopled more by southerners and were subject, in general, to a cultural environment different from that of Puritan New England.

When the Ohio and Kentucky communities were dissolved early in the present century, much of the furnishings of the dwellings and shops was dispersed, and at the present writing sources of information and authenticated western pieces are scarce as compared with the East.

The furniture in the following section is shown through the courtesy of the Warren County Historical Society, Lebanon, Ohio, and Mr. and Mrs. Robert H. Jones of The Golden Lamb Inn, Lebanon, Ohio, whose collections are also represented in the Furniture in Museum Settings Section above. The chair and detail of table illustrated below are in the Shaker Museum at Old Chatham.

Armed rocking chair from Pleasant Hill, Kentucky. In the Shaker
Museum, Old Chatham, New York.

Detail of cherry table from Pleasant Hill. One drop leaf, width 10¼″. Drawer at each end. Table is 33 inches long and 29 inches high. The top (14¾ inches wide) and leaf are one inch thick, heavier than most eastern tables. Note also the way the turning of the leg posts ends abruptly with no transition to the top of the post. Shaker Museum, Old Chatham, New York.

A Kentucky table with square tapering legs. Cherry. Height 28″,
length 53″, width 35″. From The Golden Lamb Inn.

Trestle table, walnut, from Union Village, Ohio. Height 29½″, length 73½″, width 38″. From The Golden Lamb Inn. Others like this, with marble tops, are still in use at Otterbein, Warren County, Ohio. Another dining table, with heavy trestle base and braces, from the Pleasant Hill, Kentucky, colony, was illustrated in *The Magazine Antiques* (November, 1947). The authors once owned still another, all curly maple, which was said to have originated in Union Village; though solidly constructed, it had better proportions than the Kentucky piece. A trestle table of pleasing lines is in the Shaker Museum at Auburn, Kentucky.

Cherry cupboard from Kentucky. Height 80″, length 42″, width 18″.
From The Golden Lamb Inn.

Chest of drawers, butternut, made at Union Village, Ohio, in 1827
and signed H.W.D. Warren County Museum, Lebanon, Ohio.

Hall in Center family dwelling, Pleasant Hill, Kentucky. The wall sconces, which can be adjusted to various heights, are an exclusively western device. The arched doorways are also western.

A NOTE ON SHAKER CRAFTSMEN

A chapter on the craftsmen of the sect, in our first book on Shaker furniture, listed the names of those joiners which were then known to us. Though the society took the position that principles were more important than individuals, and in fact, in the "Millennial Laws," forbade craftsmen from writing or printing their names on any article of manufacture, this was sometimes done, and in practice the worth of the individual *was* recognized.

The earlier list may now be expanded, though it is still incomplete for all the communities. The record is complicated by the fact that there was no class of furniture makers as such. Brethren skilled in working with wood might be carpenters, mechanics, coopers, makers of dippers or oval boxes, etc., as well as joiners: there were many versatile artisans in the order who could turn their hands to many trades. Such competence is illustrated in the records on "joinery" and carpentry at New Lebanon kept by Isaac N. Youngs of that community.* Following is Youngs' list of the early craftsmen and their active periods:

William Safford	(1788? – 1813)
Park Avery	(1788? – 1791)
Daniel Hilt	(1788? – 1798)
Richard Treat	(1796? – 1812)
John Bruce	(1813? – 1829)
Bushnel Fitch	(1813? – 1816)
Anthony Brewster	(1818 – 1837)
Elisha Blakeman	(1839 – 1844)
Braman Wicks	(1843 – 1847)
Orren Haskins	(1833 – 1841)

In March, 1838, Samuel Turner, Henry Bennet, and Stephen Munson were in the joiners' shop.

Makers of oval boxes:

Elder John Farrington	(c.1800)
Joseph Green	(c.1800)

*MS. in New York State Library.

102

Elder Ebenezer Cooley   (1806 – 1816)
Samuel Spier, Benjamin Lyon, and others.

Makers of dippers:

The first was Elder Abiathar Babbit, who followed the
business prior to 1811.

Even this list is not complete, however. Youngs was chiefly interested, it seems, in the artisans of the First or Senior Order, which
was only one of the eight families at New Lebanon. He makes no mention of a certain David Rowley, who "made two dining tables" at the
Church on February 24, 1838; of the first chairmakers at the East or
Hill family, probably Thomas Estes and William Thresher; or of Robert
Wagan, who, in association with Daniel Hawkins, George O. Donnell,
and others, greatly expanded the chair industry at the Second and South
families during the last half of the nineteenth century. Another South
family cabinetmaker was Erastus Rude, who was said to have been
making grandfather clock cases as early as 1806. There were certainly
other skilled joiners at the Second and North families, where some of
the finest examples of Shaker craftsmanship have been found.

Passing from New Lebanon to other communities in the East, one
is even more aware of the incompleteness of our first listing. Augustus
Grosvenor, Elijah Myrick, and Thomas Holden should be added to the
Harvard group, and Elder Philip Burlingame to the Enfield, Connecticut, chairmakers. None from Shirley have so far been identified, and
only a scattering from the other New England societies. Who, besides
David Terry, made all the lovely early chairs, tables, and sewing cabinets which have been found at Hancock? Who was responsible for the
craftsmanship at Enfield, New Hampshire, one of the most active of the
eastern societies? Maine, where there were two colonies, is so far represented by only two joiners, John Coffin and Otis Sawyer. And in New
York, since Calvin Wells and Benjamin Youngs were chiefly clockmakers, only one craftsman, Abram Ellis (Allis), is listed at Watervliet,
a productive source of fine furniture.

Ohio and Kentucky also remain open for further research. Who
were the brethren who filled the needs of the six communities in those
states? We have referred to a Timothy Bonel, who was making "chairs
and wheels" at Union Village in 1834. Another craftsman was the

talented and influential scholar and leader, Richard McNemar (1770-1839), whose remarkable career embraced all the western settlements, but particularly those at Union Village, Whitewater, and Watervliet in Ohio. In *A Sketch of the Life and Labors of Richard McNemar* (Franklin, Ohio, 1905) J. P. MacLean noted that "in handicraft but few excelled him":

> As a mechanic he could construct a lathe, make a chair, bind a book or weave cloth. From November 15th, 1813, to December, 1817, he manufactured 757 chairs, 20 big wheels, 20 little wheels, 20 reels, besides spools and whorls. Up to April 15th, 1820, he had made 1366 chairs and from that time until May, 1821, the number was 1463.

In 1837, two years before his death Elder Richard was still busy in his shop: "Some printing, some book binding, but principally chair making."

That there were other joiners in the West goes without saying. Union Village, with six families, had a larger total membership than either New Lebanon or Watervliet, New York. Pleasant Hill and South Union, in Kentucky, had many families and consequently many dwellings to furnish.

Scanning the lists already compiled one notes that many of the Shaker joiners were elders and sometimes members of the ministry. Charged with the spiritual welfare of their family or community, these leaders had risen on the basis of merit, and also, as a condition of their appointment, their having "gained a gift"—the gift of humility—in hand labor. If they became ministers they lived in the meetinghouse and worked, when official duties permitted, in a separate "ministry shop." Undoubtedly these leaders, the makers of laws and exemplars of conduct, set standards of workmanship followed by all the members of the brotherhood.

We once owned a small pine chest of drawers signed by "Father" Joseph Meacham, successor to Ann Lee and James Whittaker and organizer of the Shaker system of communitarianism. It was he, we have noted, who prescribed that "all work done, or things made in the Church for their own use ought to be faithfully and well done, but plain and without superfluity."

SUGGESTED READING

For historical background:

NOYES, JOHN HUMPHREY. *History of American Socialisms.* Philadelphia, 1870.

NORDHOFF, CHARLES. *The Communistic Societies of the United States.* New York, 1875.

HINDS, WILLIAM ALFRED. *American Communities.* Oneida, N.Y., 1878.

MELCHER, MARGUERITE FELLOWS. *The Shaker Adventure.* Princeton, N.J., 1941.

BESTOR, ARTHUR EUGENE, JR. *Backwoods Utopias.* Philadelphia, 1950.

EGBERT, DONALD DREW, AND STOW PERSONS (eds.). *Socialism and American Life.* Princeton, N.J., 1952 (Vol. I).

ANDREWS, EDWARD DEMING. *The People Called Shakers.* New York, 1953; reprinted, 1963.

DESROCHE, HENRI. *Les Shakers Americains.* Paris, 1955.

On Shaker craftsmanship:

ANDERSON, JOHN M. "Force and Form: the Shaker intuition of simplicity," *Journal of Religion,* 30 (1950).

ANDREWS, EDWARD DEMING. *The Community Industries of the Shakers.* Albany, 1933.

————"Designed for Use: The Nature of Function in Shaker Craftsmanship," *New York History,* XXXI, No. 3 (July, 1950). Cooperstown, N.Y.

ANDREWS, EDWARD DEMING AND FAITH. *Shaker Furniture: The Craftsmanship of an American Communal Sect.* Yale University Press, New Haven, 1937; reprinted: Yale, 1939; Dover Publications, Inc., N.Y., 1950, 1963.

COOMARASWAMY, ANANDA K. "Shaker Furniture," *The Art Bulletin,* XXI (1939). Chicago.

DYER, WALTER A. "The Furniture of the Shakers: A plea for its preservation as part of our national inheritance," *House Beautiful,* May, 1929.

HARRIS, A. (AMANDA) B. "Among the Shakers," *The Granite Monthly,* I, No. 1 (April, 1877). Dover, N.H.

KOUWENHOVEN, JOHN A. *Made in America: The Arts in Modern Civilization.* Garden City, New York, 1948 (Chapter 5).

MCCAUSLAND, ELIZABETH. "The Shaker legacy," *The Magazine of Art,* XXXVII (December, 1944). Washington, D.C.

MERTON, THOMAS. "The Shakers: American celibates and craftsmen who 'danced' in the glory of God," *Jubilee* (January, 1964).

O'BRIEN, HARRIET E. *Lost Utopias*. Boston, 1929 (Chapter on Shaker House).

REICHARD, GLADYS A. "Craftsmanship and Folklore," *Journal of American Folk-Lore*, 53 (1940).

ROURKE, CONSTANCE. *The Roots of American Culture*. New York, 1942 (Chapter on The Shakers).